HOW TO DRAW & PAINT FROM NATURE

CONTENTS

Introduction

LEARNING HOW TO draw and paint from the example and work of other artists has a long tradition, stretching back into prehistoric times. The earliest known examples are to be found in the cave paintings of southern France and Spain. The artists involved in making these images of bison and other game certainly learned their craft from example and no one would have been better qualified to give this than their more experienced elders.

The process has continued over the centuries, even though the demands of art have naturally changed. In the Middle Ages, for instance, the Church was the dominant influence on the artist, who spent much of his working life creating images to illustrate Biblical legends. Primitive man, on the other hand, probably painted as a type of magical process, hunting the beasts captured successfully on cave walls as a preparation for the actual events of the hunt. Between these two extremes came many others, from the decoration of buildings to the gratification of aristocratic whims. But, within all these approaches, there is a common core – the interpretation of the visual world.

Learning to see

Painting and drawing are an extension of the art of seeing. It therefore follows that learning to look and see in an aware, intelligent manner is a prerequisite of good picture making. When the first attempts to draw a portrait or paint a still life prove unsatisfactory, this is just as likely to be the result of inadequate initial observation as the result of a lack of knowledge of the actual practical techniques. In any event, the cultivation of a vision of the world about you is a most rewarding and exciting experience, as well as a yardstick against which to measure the success or failure of drawings or paintings. In undertaking the process, you will be in the company of artists throughout the centuries. All of them have learned to interpret the visual world through painstaking looking, as well as through the development of basic technical skills. Study the world about you; observe the relationships of colors and the scale of things one to another – large to small, grand to insignificant. Look also at the way artists of the past saw and painted what they observed.

This process, of necessity, must be a subjective one, even though we are all part of an endless stream of development and much common ground exists from which we can learn. What will be a 'good' picture to one artist will not necessarily be so to another; a careful depiction in great detail of a favourite landscape, for instance, will be beautiful to some, but anathema to others. However, as long as the essential discipline of looking, seeing, and interpreting is observed, the basic foundations are laid for future development. The initial technological steps themselves are not always easy – and certainly can be frustrating – but it is surprising how soon the combination of a cultivated eye and a learning hand make improvements.

The eventual rewards of making telling, well-drawn and constructed drawings and paintings are great. Much pleasure and endless joy to others can ensue; the greater your experience and the wider the range of projects undertaken, the better the results. Another great benefit that springs from picture making is that you soon learn to see the world in different ways from others. The dull, olive green tone of a tree in the foreground, alongside the acid yellow greens of fresh spring foliage, will be seen to contrast well with the sunbathed sea, shimmering turquoise blue in the middle distance. So much more can be gleaned from seeing in this way than by a casual observer.

Learning by example

There is nothing casual, however, in preparing to make such a picture work. In the example above, the artist would distance himself from the subject and study it in terms of form, color, and inter-relationships of shapes and volumes before making even an initial mark on the board or canvas.

It would be obviously foolish to be categorical about what constitutes a sensitive line, or what makes a beautiful color harmony. These are things to be discovered out of the individual qualities of the artist. The work of the great masters of the past naturally shows such individuality and another common way of learning is to study how such artists made their pictures. Try and probe beneath the surface and discover the analytical processes and personal language at work.

Visits to galleries and, if possible, to artists' studios are always helpful. In addition, copying existing works of art can provide an invaluable insight into the mind of the original painter. This system has been used as a method of art education for a very long time. Even well-established artists both in the past and in the present make copies; indeed, the only surviving record of some very early pictures is through the copies made by later artists. Rubens (1577–1640), for instance, copied carefully a Leonardo da Vinci (1452–1519) mural. The original has long since disappeared and the work is known today only through the copy.

Often, the techniques used in the original will reveal themselves to you in making your own version of the painting or drawing. Discovering the way color is balanced, lines are put together across the canvas, perspective is drawn and character delineated will not only add to your experience but reflect back into your own work.

Constructing a picture

When constructing a picture – constructing is the most appropriate word to describe the process – always remember that the single most important factor at the outset is the support you choose, whether it is paper, board, or canvas. The shape is significant because different shapes and proportions engender different emotions and moods. Thus a square will convey stability and solidity, while a long, narrow rectangle will suggest calm. Such horizontal rectangles are referred to as 'landscape' and vertical ones as 'portrait'. These two terms should not be confused with areas of

Left: Some of the earliest examples of drawing and painting are found in the caves of southern France. These images of bison and hunters were thought to have magical powers which promised success and prosperity.
Below: Peter Paul Rubens, 'The Judgement of Paris'. The 16th century artist Rubens was a master at rendering the figure and is well known for his fleshy, opulent nudes.

work. Constable (1776–1837), for instance, painted many landscapes on vertical canvases, while Degas (1834–1917) painted portraits on horizontal ones.

The next important consideration is the suitability of the support's surface for the selected medium, technique, and subject. A finely smoothed surface on a stable base, either of wood or millboard, with a prepared priming to allow oil paint to be laid on it is essential for small, detailed paintings. A canvas with a medium coarse texture, stretched on to a stretching frame, will prove suitable for either one of two completely different approaches. The canvas can be used for thinly 'scumbled' areas, which will allow the warp and the weft of the texture to show through, or for larger and broader styles of painting, with plenty of 'fat' in the paint.

The intention of the picture – whether it is to suggest a strong sense of vigour, atmosphere, or great fidelity to the carefully observed subject – must first be decided upon, since the choice of actual working materials stems from it, together with the techniques employed. Remember, for instance, that not all painters use brushes exclusively. The palette knife, rag, and even fingers have long been part of the stock-in-trade of the artist.

When choosing the scale for a painting or drawing, be guided by the demands of the subject. Pencil portraits, for instance, are usually better at, or below, life size; the problems that may be encountered if the scale is increased can be formidable. Again, however, such a general rule can be broken, if the nature of the work demands it.

Every individual demand will conjure up an individual solution – a compound of all that has been learned from observation, experience, and the study of other works. Rough and smooth, tightly finished or very loosely suggested, in pencil, chalk, oil, tempera, watercolor, or pen and ink – the choice is there to be made and the factors governing the decision can be rapidly assessed. Nor should the opportunity for experiment be ignored, even at an initial stage. It is always worth trying a few variations in both techniques and media. For example, try making a still life in color – say, in gouache – and in black-and-white, perhaps using graphite powder and a soft, finely sharpened pencil.

The criterion for anything you may produce should be quality. If color is involved, then it should be harmonious, or disruptive by choice, not by accident. Balance should be aimed for in the design, but it should satisfy the viewer's need for completeness. Areas of relative inactivity can be balanced against small, tightly focused areas, where a great deal is happening. Dimensional suggestion is a further important element. The use of linear perspective and what is called atmosphere, or 'aerial perspective', to create illusions of space will also bring rewards from applied study.

Oil painting

Oil paint is perhaps the commonest and most popular painting medium in current use. Its flexibility and potential range is legion. Brought into use on a wide scale by the Flemish brothers Hubert and Jan Van Eyck in the 15th century, oil paint gradually superseded the less flexible medium of tempera, which had been in common use before.

It was discovered that, when oil was added to the tempera, the result was a richer, brighter effect. The use of the new medium soon spread, particularly in 15th century Venice, where oils were found to be far more suitable for the city's humid atmosphere than tempera had been.

The earliest oil paintings were made on wooden panels with a specially treated surface. This was achieved by coating the panels with several thin skins of size – rabbit-skin glue or a similar product – and then covering them with a ground. Often, gesso was used for the purpose. This consisted of a mixture of size and whiting or chalk. Several coats in total were applied, each individual coat being rubbed smooth before another layer was applied. The finished surface would then be highly polished to render it only slightly absorbent – just enough to allow the paint to bond to it, but not enough to let the color go 'flat'. This term describes what happens when the ground tends to suck the color in, leaving the surface dull. Sometimes, this can be deliberately cultivated as part of a technique, but, in general, it should be avoided – at least in the initial stages – because it is very difficult to control.

From panels to canvas
The original panels, however, soon proved unsuitable for many paintings since their rigidity made them liable to split when subjected to extreme temperature or atmospheric changes. At this point, the idea of painting on canvas – a woven surface made from flax stretched across a frame, originated. The advantages of this new method were immediately apparent as material thus suspended will stretch and shrink within tolerable limits to accommodate the changes the panels rejected.

Initially, the surface was prepared in much the same way that the wooden panels had been. But, before long, variations developed as the result of artistic experiment and demand.

Primers and grounds
It soon became clear to the early oil painters that, while white was a useful background for many subjects, it was not necessarily the most suitable surface for all of them. Accordingly, colored or tinted grounds were soon introduced and the range of options open to painters thus expanded. The painters of 15th century Florence – Botticelli (1444–1510), Michelangelo (1475–1564) and Leonardo da Vinci – worked on a cool green base, the quality of which is reflected in their finished paintings. Because these artists tended to use descriptive local color – that is, the approximate blue for sky, green for grass, pink for flesh and so on – the effect was cool. This added to the overall calmness and dignity of the finished pictures.

The Venetian artists of the same period, on the other hand, used a strong red-brown underpainting with startlingly different results. Painters such as Bellini (1400–70), Titian (c.1487–1576), Giorgione (1477–1510) and Veronese (1528–88) used reflective color, the summary of all the various touches of color which strike the surface of the objects being painted, to arrive at an apparently descriptive color.

The painting technique employed by the Venetians was similarly different from that of their Florentine counterparts since it tended to be less linear. This term is used to describe a work in which the shapes are defined with finite edges – one edge meeting the other – with the objects themselves being filled in with modulated tones of color. In the alternative system, as practiced by the Venetians, the edges tend to run into each other. The lines, far from being precise, are frequently

Jan van Eyck, 'Man
in a Turban'. Van
Eyck is purported to
have been one of the
earliest oil painters;
before his time
tempera was the
most common
medium. The
techniques used are
similar to tempera.

ing. A battleship grey, for instance, may well create a flat, uninteresting overall mood; a scarlet or crimson will make the work unbearably hot and brash. Often a thin wash of a neutral warm tone, say an earth color, such as raw sienna, will prove highly suitable.

Types and mediums

Oil paint is fundamentally a fusion of powdered pigments derived from both organic and man-made substances. These are mixed with an oil to dilute them to a consistency suitable for painting. The method of manufacture has varied little over the centuries. The grinding and emulsifying of pigment, which was the task of apprentice painters in the Renaissance, is essentially the same process as the one used in the commercial manufacturers of today.

The agent used to adapt the paint from the stiff, pure state in which it leaves the tube to the workable, viable condition needed for actual painting is called the medium. In the case of oil paint, the medium is invariably an oil, more usually a mixture of oils.

The test of time has shown that pure spirits of turpentine is a useful dilutant. However, because turpentine has a different drying rate to the heavier oils used in manufacturing the paint, it evaporates more quickly. It is advisable, therefore, to mix it with another substance to delay the process.

Linseed oil is the most suitable for this. Its use allows much more elasticity in the colors laid on the picture, i prevents cracking and also leaves color values more apparent and fresh. Poppy oil is preferred by some artists, just as stand oil is used if its own particular characteristics of rich and fatty surface marks are required. Some artists, too, like to use turpentine mixed with a varnish, though the latter is usually reserved for glazing the actual picture.

The paints themselves are made in various qualities. Inexpensive paints are usually ground into an oil that is known to darken with time and exposure to light. The fine, expensive, permanent types used by professionals are always ground into the best available oils; they also consist of the finest stable and well-balanced pigments.

The painter's palette

When selecting paints, it is advisable to limit the range of colors on the

broken and ragged. The latter technique is much closer to the way the human retina receives an image; color signals reach the brain and dance back and forth to arrive at a consensus of color.

Colored or tinted canvases are just as useful to the artists of today as they were for the artists who first devised them. They allow artists to keep tight control of the organization of the design and particularly of the tonal structure. This describes the light, dark, and mid-tone range of colors used within the work. The theoretical extremes of this are black at one end and white at the other, though, in practice, it is likely to be far more subtle.

The tonal structure is an integral part of what is termed 'painting the lights' – that is, working up from a dark ground to the mid-tones and, finally, the highlights. When embarking on this process, remember that certain tones tend to deaden a paint-palette as many of the more esoteric and arcane formulae are unnecessary. Learning to cope with such a restriction will reap dividends later. The great artists of the past prided themselves on their ability to create a complete range of colors from a very limited palette and there is no reason why contemporary artists should not follow their example.

One suggested palette for painting figures or portraits from life would be flake or titanium white, yellow ochre, light red, terre verte, raw umber, and cobalt blue. By careful mixing and experiment, mixing these colors together in varying proportions will create a great range of shades, all sympathetic to the rippling feeling of live flesh.

It will be noted that no strong color is present in this suggested palette. If, however, it is necessary to intensify a local color, such as lipstick, rouge, or the lighter tone of gold earrings, cadmium red or alizarin crimson can be employed, together with chromium or chrome yellow.

Always feel free to experiment, but bear in mind that the so-called 'fugitive' colors and inflexible ready-made tints should be avoided. Fugitive colors are so-named because they fade when exposed to light; they can also be destroyed chemically when mixed with certain other colors. It is advisable to check the lists supplied by all reputable art stores. These use a coded system to grade paint permanence, based on the durability, reliability and relative instability of the

colors. But the best insurance against all possible trouble is to buy the very best that can be afforded in the first place.

Painting techniques

The techniques of oil painting enable a vast range of varied effects and textures to be created. For example scumbling or glazing with the same color can produce quite different effects within the same picture.

In scumbling, thickish paint is rubbed into the surface, with the result that it tends to pick up the texture of the support. Glazing is a technique often incorporated with others and is particularly effective for painting flesh. The system is based on laying skins of color, like washes, over a light ground – frequently white.

Each glaze qualifies earlier ones; the result is rich, transparent, and glowing. Preserving this transparent colour quality is one of the fundamental aims of glazing and it helps if a means can be found to accelerate the drying time. Note, too, that when thin washes of paint are applied, the painting must be laid flat, as otherwise they would drip across the surfaces.

Under no circumstances should a turpentine substitute be used for glazing. Because the molecular structure of the oils used in such substitutes does not marry with those used in the paints, the result can be disastrous. Substitutes should be employed only as solvents to clean brushes, clear palettes, wipe up drops of spilled paint and the like.

Stick to pure distilled spirts of turpentine when actually painting. indeed, the same principle applies – the best possible materials produce the best results.

Acrylics

Acrylics were invented in response to the pressing need for a flexible paint, capable of retaining its brilliance when exposed to the open air. They are made from pigment ground into either an acrylic resin or polyvinyl acetate. The paints dry quickly because they are water-soluble; the factor governing the drying rate is the time it takes the water to evaporate. This means that an artist can repaint or overpaint much more quickly than with oils.

The paints have other advantages as well. They possess great permanence as their chemical structure makes them resist oxidization and decomposition, while each layer bonds permanently to the preceding one.

Sometimes the quick drying time can be a disadvantage. In such cases, a retarding agent can be added to slow down the process and so allow time for adjustments to the painting to be made while the surface is still wet.

Tools and techniques

The nature of acrylics means that a wide range of tools can be used to apply them. Conventional brushes are excellent; working with a palette knife will produce the same striking results as it will with oils. Rags and sponges will work well too. Techniques are similarly varied, the range of options matching the thickness or immediate thinness of the paint being used.

An interesting technique – between traditional watercolor and oil painting – is to glaze over a thick base, which can be either wet or dry. Use a sponge or a rag. Again, the key is to experiment and so discover the best ways of exploiting the true characteristics of the paint. Start with traditional methods, underpainting in thin, flowing washes with a tendency to monochrome, and from this move on to scratching back, glazing over, and blotting.

Watercolor

Watercolor is the most suitable medium for working outside the studio. Its characteristics are quite distinct from those of oils and need careful study in order to exploit them

Sandro Botticelli, 'Virgin and Child with St John and Angel'. The artist Botticelli was one of the most influential painters of 15th century Florence and his linear lyricism epitomizes the elegance found in paintings of this period. Madonna paintings were very popular during this time and Botticelli grew prosperous and well-known for paintings similar to the one shown here. The circular shape of the surface adds a feeling of symmetry and peace; however, even without this, the painting would be harmonious and balanced.

Michelangelo
Buonarroti, 'The
Manchester
Madonna'. This
painting is
interesting not only
for its compositional
excellence, but
because it illustrates
15th century
painting techniques.
Note the use of terre
verte for flesh tones.

fully. The prime quality of watercolor is its transparency. It makes more use of the support – usually paper of one type and texture or another – by allowing it to shine through the thin, watered paint skins and also to describe the white, or near white, colors in the picture. This contrasts totally with the technique of working 'to the lights' used in oil painting. Because of the need to make decisions before applying the paint, it means that a great deal of discipline and organization is required, as opposed to other methods of painting.

The medium itself is an extremely old one. Frescoes, for example, are actually a form of watercolor, while watercolors on paper were being created long before the medium became popular in the 18th and 19th centuries. Part of this popularity sprang from the introduction of commercial watercolors in the 1700s. The process of manufacture itself is simple; the colors are simply powdered pigments ground in with gum arabic. Since the original method was invented, various other additives have been introduced, but, though these have been found to be effective, the established formula remains the original one.

Nevertheless, the flowering of watercolor remains linked inevitably with the birth of the great watercolorist tradition in 18th century England. Artists such as John Cotman (1782–1842) and William Turner (1775–1851) brought the technique to extremely high levels. One of the more interesting elements is the scale and sense of space they achieved, given the limitation of the size of their canvases.

Most watercolor paintings are small – primarily because of the need for portability, but also due to other factors. The size of a painting is always directly related to the size of the average mark made with the medium in use. With watercolor, because of its relatively rapid drying time and the optimum amount of paint that can be carried by the brush, the commonest size is about 20in (50cm) by 30in (65cm). However, many of the finest examples are considerably smaller than this.

It was the artists of this period, too, who developed the classical watercolour method. This is to stretch the paper first by soaking it in clean water and then, while still wet, taping it firmly to a support, on which it is allowed to dry and tighten. This not only eliminates wrinkles and other surface blemishes; it also lifts off any grease that might be on it, via fingerprints, for instance.

Techniques and toning

Artists of the past decided upon the mood of the scene they were painting in advance and toned their paper accordingly. This general principle is a helpful one to follow, since it serves to blend the various elements of the picture together. If the scene is to be bright, sunlit and cheerful, a very light wash of Naples yellow or yellow ochre could be used; if a heavier, overcast mood is required, a thin wash of Payne's grey or another neutral blue grey could be employed. Through this, any subsequent color will be slightly modified in tone, though not enough to prevent anything left as white appearing as white.

Most artists find the assessment and organization of tone to be the most difficult aspect of watercolor painting and, to cope with the difficulty, resort to many devices, including the squint and the white paper viewfinder. Squinting results in a stronger definition of tonal contrasts, with mid-darks becoming darker and lights remaining strongly light. A viewfinder helps not only in ascertaining the related tones, but also the composition of the picture.

A small rectangle – the same proportion as the picture surface – is cleanly cut out of a sheet of stiff white paper. By holding it at arm's length, or closer, and closing one eye, the range of possibilities of relating objects to the picture edge can be determined. By this means, for instance, a cropped part of a tuft of grass in the foreground can be rapidly contrasted with its effect on the whole picture.

Colors are laid over the carefully organized tonal base from a limited range and in varying densities. A mellow olive green, for example, would cover most of the foliage, creating both a sense of unity and establishing the color idea. Adjustments are always made during the course of work; the answer is not simply to remove an inconvenient tree or reduce the height of a hill to make the scene tell. The whole aim is to organize the colors into an arrangement that is at once atmospheric and descriptive. Indeed, some artists believe that the melting of colors into one another is as important a part of watercolor as the quality of transparency.

Gouache

Gouache, or body color, is included within the broad definition of watercolor. It is a water-based paint, usually made of coarsely ground pigments, but instead of having the distinctively transparent quality of pure watercolor, it is opaque.

Many techniques can be used with gouache, but a number share common ground with watercolor, oils and tempera. It should never be used as a substitute, however, since it possesses its own potential and beauty.

Using gouache on a dampened ground, for instance, creates interesting effects, as it is possible to use overlays to obliterate or qualify earlier marks. Floating semi-transparent details into a picture broadly sketched in colored inks can create a unique atmosphere, with the artist being able to use gouache alongside watercolor to contrast the latter's transparency with solid color touches. Ordinary watercolor mixed with strong opaque white can produce a similar effect.

Tempera

Before the advent of oils, tempera was the main medium for easel pictures – small, compact works in contrast to the huge frescoes decorating the walls of medieval churches. It still enjoys a good deal of popularity, deservedly so for its surface and color qualities are extremely fine. It also has the advantage of being easily produced – a few simple ingredients plus a little labor produce a full range of colors.

The basis of tempera is fresh egg, which is used to emulsify finely ground pigments. Some artists prefer to use only the yolk; others use the whole egg. Oil can also be blended into the simple mixture in order to achieve an additional quality. It is vital that the eggs are completely fresh; any unused mixture must be thrown away at the end of the day. If old yolks are used – even one day later – the paint will go bad. All tools – knives, pestle and mortar, glass sheet and so on – used to produce the paint must be kept scrupulously clean. Failure to do so will encourage moulds to grow on the painted surface.

Different tempera mixtures produce very different effects. Some tempera tends to look flat and gouache-like, while others are much more resonant and brilliant. The purest form is the mixture of egg yolk, pigment, and distilled water; this is permanent, virtually insoluble and inexpensive.

Supports and techniques

Suitable supports include wood and millboard panels. These are especially satisfctory when primed with several coats of gesso and then buffed to produce a highly smoothed surface. The range of techniques that can be employed is very wide indeed, due partly to the rapid drying time. Strangely enough, the home-made variety tends to dry faster than proprietory tubed brands. Skimming color thinly, flooding it in washes, stippling, splattering, glazing are all possibilities.

Tempera's flexibility also makes it suitable for painting a wide range of subjects. There is a long tradition of portrait and figure painting in the medium; it has been used, too, for landscapes, still life, and natural history subjects. The aim should always be to produce the typical tempera qualities of quietness and softness of colour and feeling.

Drawing

The idea conjured up by the word 'drawing' is invariably of pencil marks made on a sheet of white paper. 'Pencil', therefore, is synonymous with drawing in most peoples' minds. That this should be so, although not by any means entirely true, is understandable. For many years pencil has been found to be the most sympathetic and subtly variable instrument for documenting, describing and analysing an image.

The Italian masters of the 15th century were all familiar with silverpoint, a stick of silver sharpened to a point. Silverpoint was used to enable the artist to build up a continuous tone of great sensitivity. In the past, silverpoint drawing was done on a specially prepared sheet of colored paper.

Chalk was also a forerunner of the present day pencil and had greater immediacy and fluency than the quieter quality of silverpoint. Most chalk studies were the raw material for subsequent paintings. Indeed, these studies often remained in a master's studio for years, being used in several works and often inherited by students for use in later pictures.

Silverpoint was suitable for deliberate and careful investigation while chalk increased the range of activity.

Jean August Ingres, 'Pencil Study'. Ingres was extremely adept at simple pencil studies of this sort. Using only a rough outline and areas of shading, Ingres captured his subject with economy.

With chalk the outlines of a proposed composition and the perspective necessary to locate figures within the implied space could be worked out.

Pencil types and supports

Attention should be paid to the broad range of marks available with the pencil from the fine incisive line of a hard lead, to the thick crumbling smudges created by a heavy black lead. Pencils are produced in varying degrees of hardness and a grading system is employed by manufacturers to identify these grades. The 'H' series are the hardest and the range progresses down to the 8B – an extremely soft lead. The combination of different grades of mark within one picture is very effective, as in the combination of detailing with a 4H to broad, richly rendered and freely applied tones with a 4 or 6B.

The range of pencil types does not end there; wax pencils, charcoal pencils, conté crayons and several others all have their own unique qualities to exploit, combine, and experiment with.

The support used for working in

Edgar Degas, 'Woman Drying Herself'. Degas was one of the great innovators and promoters of pastels. He experimented widely with different techniques and developed a 'painting' method which involved spraying the pastel surface with warm water or milk. Degas' use of gesture and color are important aspects to study. He was also one of the first artists to use broken color – strokes of pure color which 'mix' optically. Many of the Impressionists incorporated his discoveries in their work.

pencil is very important since the quality of the drawing will always be dependent upon the texture and tone of the paper or board used. A hard pencil will make a strong dark line on a rough textured paper, just as a soft lead will make a fine and crisp line on a smoother surface.

Drawing techniques and mixed media
The smudge, and tones comprising linear marks rather like those described in the comments on silverpoint drawing, are all part of the range of techniques possible with the pencil.

The pencil is very effective when used in combination with other media – both water and oil based – and can be drawn on to canvas and gesso grounds, as well as paper. A relatively recent development worth exploiting are colored pencils. Used either as full color to describe things as seen, or to introduce color suggestions into a pencil drawing, they are equally effective. Colored pencils are also likely to be affected by the texture of the paper

and so the issue of scale is obviously important.

The drawing process
A sound way to learn to render the form and volume in, say, a figure study, is to work in a pencil with a very hard lead on a large, smoothish piece of paper. By this means, if the paper measures about 20in × 30in (50cm × 65cm), the amount of labour needed to make the marks of, say, a 2H pencil show on the surface, allows the artist to scratch away and correct mistakes without the faults needing the use of an eraser. If erasing can be avoided, one can learn from these corrections, for by seeing the 'false' lines left alongside their more accurate brethren, fewer uncertainties should occur.

Pastels

Pastels share some of the characteristics of both painting and drawing media. The sticks, made from finely

powdered pigment and a surprisingly small amount of gum or resin, have been in use for many years. They produce a characteristic powdery quality, which many artists find extremely attractive.

Because the great majority of pastels have an opaque nature, the papers and boards commonly used with them tend to be toned or colored. Many artists prefer to tone their own surfaces, particularly if textured ones are being used. Their use is often combined with charcoal or black chalk; the latter are harder and so introduce a tough, energetic linear quality, which contrasts well with the soft, blended feeling generally associated with the pure pastel.

Techniques
By experimenting with the widest possible range of marks, surfaces, and techniques, it will become apparent that there is an optimum size, style and feeling for working in pastel. A warm, hot, or cool-toned paper

or board, for instance, will produce an entirely different mood and spirit in the eventual work. Roughly applying pastel to coarse paper, or finely smoothing pastels to a fine surface, will have similarly differing effects.

One method of working is to use pastel to render the subject to a highly finished state and then to flood water or milk across the surface. This melts the tones together to form a 'painted' finished picture. The technique was employed by Edgar Degas (1834–1917) and others. Degas used pastel throughout his life to produce some of his most celebrated works. From the briefest of sketches to formal compositions, he was a master of the medium.

Another popular and successful method of working in pastel is a technique known as 'working the lights'. In this, the main structures and features of the painting are ticked in on a toned ground in soft pencil and then the light tones and colors are carefully defined, using light pastels. These will be later developed into the middle and dark tones; here, a torchon, a roll of paper used to blend colours together, can be extremely useful.

A knowledge of 'gesture' is as important in pastel as in all other media. As defined in art practice, gesture means the type of marks made by the individual artist on the surface. The gesture can be long and lingering or short and staccato, depending on the medium, the size of the subject, and the subject matter itself. Experience is the key factor; in pastel, the stroke of the broad side of the stick or the softened finger-rubbed mark will both contribute to the quality of the image. The trick is knowing when to use which technique.

Oil pastel

The oil pastel is a relatively recent innovation. This is a stick of color, similar to the traditional pastel, but instead consisting of oil-bound pigment in a solid form. It behaves in a very different way to orthodox pastels and should be exploited for its own distinct characteristics.

Since oil pastels are inclined to be more clumsy than 'pure' pastel, it is best to use them on a small scale. The images they produce are fluid and malleable and, as an ingredient in mixed media painting, they have proved themselves able to create a wide range of effects. One technique is to lay in the broad, general outlines of composition and color harmonies in oil pastel and then overpaint in gouache. If the oil rejects the gouache, a little soft soap can be added to the paint to enable it to cover the pastels effectively.

An attractive result can be achieved from a technique based upon an old method called 'wash off'. Lay in the broad basic composition and block in the main colors with oil pastels. Work up details in colored inks and gouache, leaving occasional gaps between the features within the piece. When dry, cover the whole work with a coat of white gouache, applying this thickly enough to create a solid sheet of color. of colour.

Carefully spread a further coat of black waterproof India ink over the gouache and allow it to dry completely. Beneath the resulting black surface will be the original design waiting to be revealed. By scraping across the black, inked surface with the flat of a single-edged razor blade, or a similar sharp instrument, the layers beneath will emerge in varying degrees.

Pen and ink

There is a long tradition of pen and ink drawing, its particular incisiveness being found useful for recording fine detail. The studies for the major works executed by Michelangelo and others include a number of pen and ink studies.

With the invention of photo-mechanical methods of printing, the pen and ink drawing has taken on a completely new significance, and we now live in the long shadow of its influence. For the first time, pen and ink is no longer being used for the planning of larger and more significant work, but is used to create the finished work itself.

Prior to the invention of photo-mechanical printing, the draftsman drew the image on to wooden blocks. These were then engraved by superlative craftsmen so well that the resultant woodblock, ready for printing in the books and magazines of the time, almost totally simulated the character of the original drawing. However, because of the timely and costly process of engraving in this way and the necessarily static feeling imparted to the finished work, it was difficult to transmit the calligraphic feel in the original drawing.

Much finer lines, with closer interstices are possible than those seen in such results; melting the edges of lines by drawing on to dampened paper, rubbing the still wet ink to contrast with the sharper drawn lines will create and suggest further possibilities.

Pen types and supports
Pens are made in a wide variety of

Honoré Daumier, 'The Wayside Railway Station'. Daumier's pictures are unique in their ability to evoke atmosphere and mood. He often used the working classes as subjects for his paintings and drawings.

13

Michelangelo Buonarotti, 'Studies'. The pen and ink studies of Michelangelo are an excellent way for the artist to study the use of line to create tone and structure.

it back and draw in a small portion over the pencil marks in pen and ink. Follow this by again folding the top sheet down on to the absorbent paper and rub gently over the back in the location of the freshly drawn ink marks, thus transferring it in reverse on to the other surface. Continue this process through until the whole image is transferred.

This technique is of interest not only in its own right but also in combination with others. Traditionally, pen and ink has been used in association with washes of diluted inks and line reinforcing broad masses of simple tones. Splattering tone across and into dry and wet pen and ink lines is one technique, and the use of masking devices to prevent them is another.

Colored inks
As in the case of colored pencils, the range of colored inks is now a part of the artist's repertoire, and a relatively recent phenomena. If used as part of a technique including black and white, these inks are interesting; however, attention should be drawn to the extremely fugitive nature of the color and their tendency to fade with time. Because of this, it is preferable to avoid combining colored inks into pictures to be considered otherwise permanent – e.g., gouache or watercolor.

Mixed media
Whether hatching finely or running lines freely over the page, pen and ink will respond in a great many ways. Mixed with other media, a good deal of invention can take place with colored or black ink on colored grounds; or black lines on a carefully rendered watercolor will bring forth fresh results. Combine several types of nib and brush marks. Don't forget the newer types of pen such as the rapidograph and ballpoint pens.

Erasing
To erase false marks, make sure the ink is dry and scrape gently with a knife or razor to remove the unsuccessful area. By carefully burnishing the erased area, one can render the surface suitable for redrawing.

Composition

The illustrations created by perspective systems are a major factor in constructing a good, sound composition. Composition is the term used to express organization of varied and

sizes and styles and the supports suitable are of great number. From mapping pens – extremely fine nibs developed for cartographers – to coarse steel, inflexible nibs and variations in between, all are readily available. The making of pens from quills and reeds is well worth persevering with, and varying the size of the nib will result in a great number of variations. Making use of unlikely sources for nibs is not to be discounted. Those made for use in lettering will make a mark fatter, fuller, and more flowing than most of the standard types. Again, the paper used will affect the appearance of the finished piece of work.

The range of supports does not necessarily stop with those available from the artists' supplier. Absorbent surfaces – those treated with size – are

sympathetic upon which to make certain images. Wrapping paper, blotting paper and tracing paper take the ink from the pen in entirely different ways.

Techniques
An interesting result can be achieved by making drawings by means of the offset technique. On a sheet of highly sized paper – tracing paper or similar – tick in the main points of the drawing and bring it to a finished stage with pencils. When you consider the picture ready for transfer, hinge the sheet of paper along the long edge to a sheet of blotting or semi-absorbent paper with adhesive tape. Make sure that the original drawing can be folded flat to present the entire drawing image neatly on to the other sheet. Then fold

disparate elements within the painting to create legibility and visual interest. The balance and interrelationship of lines, masses, colors, and movement are also aspects of composition.

Over the centuries, the attempt to create standards for the making of art has taken many forms from ideal proportions for drawing the human form, to systematic color patterning.

The 'ideal', as exemplified by the Greeks as the definition of perfect proportion, was based upon a theory known as the Golden Section. This is a mathematical formula by which a line is divided in such a way that the smaller part is to the larger as the larger part is to the whole. The Golden Section was considered to hold balance naturally, entirely satisfying the human eye for symmetry and harmony. Ever since this rule was proposed, geometry has been an important and recurring concept in painting and drawing.

Atmosphere can only be sustained over the whole surface by equal consideration being given to its several parts. The basic types of composition are those based on geometry which have been used for a great many years, both in the simple and more sophisticated forms. For example, often the triangular structure found in early Madonna and Child paintings will be complemented by an inverted or interrelated triangle, sometimes to an astonishingly complex degree.

Piero della Francesca (1410/20–1492) was an Italian artist as interested in mathematics as in art but the complicated compositional structures he used did not detract from the picture's beauty and compassion. Piero is considered one of the world's greatest masters and little effort is needed to see why – not only are the linear interrelationships on the picture surface highly resolved, but color is used both logically and to enhance the aims and intentions of the picture.

These compositions are distinguished by a generally static and classical mood – an inevitable outcome of the systems used. Alternative methods have long been used and the rhythmic composition of a Rubens or Delacroix show some of them in action. In order to suggest movement, or to lead the eye across the picture surface, it is necessary to achieve balance by some other means. The interlocking of the main directional lines into a satisfactory arrangement to tell

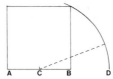

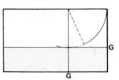

The Golden Section. This rule is ascribed to Euclid as the ideal division of a surface. Far left: To find the vertical Section, divide line AB in half to create C. Next, draw a radius from the top right corner to create D. In the next picture, draw in lines to create a rectangle. Point BG is the vertical Section. Far right: To find the horizontal Section, draw a line from the top of the vertical line G to the bottom right corner. Create a radius from the top right corner downward. Where the line and arc intersect is the horizontal Section.

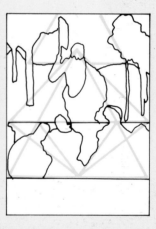

Structure. The 15th century Italian artist Piero della Francesca was as interested in geometry as in painting. Top right: The triangle is the geometric base from which Piero worked. Bottom right: Following this principle, many triangles, can be discovered.

the story use the surface and employ all available space.

The picture space

How often has one seen pictures with the interest focused in the center, leaving corners and outer edges unoccupied, or localized nests of activity with barren and uninteresting deserts of space all around? Poussin, (1594–1665) the French painter, was greatly concerned with the grammar of composition and would invite the viewer to gain by viewing beyond the focal point all parts of the canvas being used.

Dramatic gesture demands balance of an asymmetrical kind. The eye needs to make space for such implied movement, in much the same way that a profile portrait will require more space between the front of the face and edge, than between the back and parallel edges.

Dramatic impact will be enhanced within the composition by a variety in scale and to this end the exploitation of close and distant viewing, not only tonally as in atmospheric perspective, but as contrasts of size on the surface. The eye of a head in close up will be seen to be approximately the same size as the full figure at a short distance behind. A sea gull in flight above foreground cliffs will occupy the major part of the picture plane. Exploit these contrasts and use them with the other useful contributory parts.

<u>Piero di Cosimo</u>, 'The Forest Fire' Man was painting and drawing the birds and beasts of his environment long before he began to

Nature

consider himself worthy of such attention. Cosimo has here used the subject to portray many animals in a natural environment.

THE FOUNDATION OF all Western art rests upon the cave paintings of Stone Age man. Drawn, scratched and painted on the dark walls of the caves, they invariably depict the struggle for life and survival of primitive man. The hunt for food was described, man usually triumphing over his prey, be it bison or deer. These pictures were not celebrations of man's prowess and skill, but rather thanksgivings for their continued survival. These images were no doubt made to influence magical sources and thereby ensure success in the true event; a rehearsal for the subsequent performance. Whatever the reasons for their making, the quality of observation in the pictures of the animals is most impressive, and this is a characteristic that has been apparent ever since.

What was true historically is still so, that in general paintings and drawings of birds, animals and fishes are best put into a context, usually their natural habitat. Pisanello (c.1395–1456), an Italian artist, specialized in animal depictions and made fine detailed drawings of working and wild creatures. Dürer, the 16th century German master, surely surprised his audience when he made drawings of elephants and a rhinoceros! The quality of care and study in a picture like Piero Cosimos 'Forest Fire' is truly remarkable.

It is to be recommended that sketch books used in a zoo or wildlife park be used as the raw material for natural history pictures, and the opportunity to study closely any dead beast of the field or sky, whether bought from the poulterer or found by the roadside, should not be missed.

Although George Stubbs (1724–1806), an English painter who specialized in animal and landscape paintings, studied anatomy to very great lengths (even publishing an *Anatomy of the Horse*) such profound knowledge is not essential. Intelligent observation and a basic awareness of structure and limits of movement plus elementary arithmetic, will generally suffice. This is necessary because of the frustration in finding that in the full preoccupation of describing

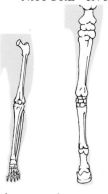

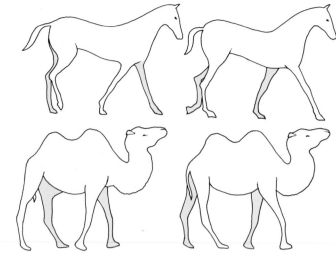

Anatomy An understanding of human and animal anatomy is a great aid for the artist. Here the leg of a human (left) is contrasted with the leg of a horse (right). Note the differences in structure and size.

Movement To accurately capture an animal in motion, the artist should study the pattern of its gait. The horse (top), depending upon its speed, moves with the legs in close conjunction. The camel (bottom) however, will always move with legs on the same side at an equal distance.

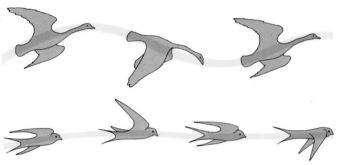

Flight Animals are rarely still and it is to the artist's advantage to study their movements. Above: the flight of a swan (top) is contrasted with that of a swallow (bottom). Note how the head and neck move in relation to the wings and the dipping motion of the swan's flight as opposed to the straight path of the swallow.

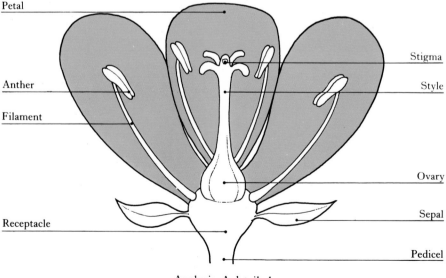

Petal

Anther

Filament

Receptacle

Stigma

Style

Ovary

Sepal

Pedicel

Analysis A detailed study of a flower is a useful exercise for the artist in gaining discipline and improved seeing.

colour, texture, and the other features of a prime specimen, one feather too many – maybe even one fin too few – may inadvertently result.

An excellent way to gain knowledge and confidence is to locate a museum with a collection of stuffed creatures. These are often mounted as tableaux with the young following the parent, or the bird of prey suspended above a suitable habitat. This information can supplement the zoo sketchbook and provide a sound base upon which to create pictures.

Much very good natural history work dealing with animal life has a spirit and vitality reflecting outdoor life in general, but other examples are mainly concerned with the intricacies and finer points of the subject. Such types of work often use natural history objects such as shells, stones, pieces of tree bark and things of that character. This will give the opportunity to exploit the contrasting of textures and colour.

In general, it is as well to consider the descriptive color of the items used in the group or scene. Most animals, eggshells, fishes, etc. have survival reasons for their coloration; camouflage, as used in wartime, is an art adapted from the animal kingdom. Color contrasts are also unique, as seen in the cock pheasant who has such strong, brightly colored feathers so as to be attractive to the hen. Indeed, in the world of birds, the difference between functional color in the male and female is very marked indeed.

Watercolor and gouache are very suitable for making notes or developing pictures of natural subjects. There are many fine examples to see from Dürer to Holman Hunt. Study the way an artist will flood basic tones and colors before finding details in more solid color. Observe the choice of background color and whether it is dark enough to give a strong feeling of the shape of the beast, or subtle enough to allow for feathers or fur to melt into it and so suggest the natural environment.

A technique that has proved useful when working in the field is to use a basic range of oils, say yellow ochre, burnt sienna, Payne's grey, cobalt blue, and a bottle of turpentine. Or, to make drawings, only a few clean rags, very soft black pencils and a small collection of oil pastels are needed. Study the movement of the creatures to be drawn in detail; if it is a tiger

Dürer, 'The Hare'.
In this exceptional
watercolor painting,
Dürer has success
fully rendered an
animal at rest.

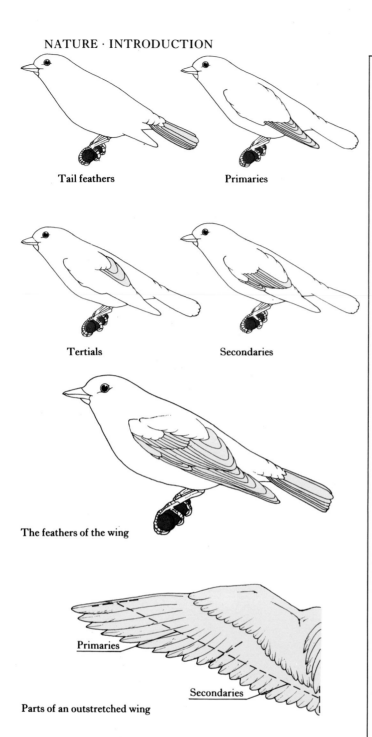

Tail feathers   Primaries

Tertials   Secondaries

The feathers of the wing

Primaries

Secondaries

Parts of an outstretched wing

walking up and down its enclosure, for instance, see at which point in his perambulations the pose is repeated. When you feel that you have engraved the main rhythms in your mind, take a little paint from a tube, dilute this with turpentine and rub on to the paper defining the general shape and color of the animal with the rag. Correct this by adding more smears of paint and when this underpainting looks convincing, draw in with black pencil all the main lines. By adding details with pencil and the oil pastels, the drawing will quickly take shape. With practice this will prove a very useful means of making notes and recording movements.

Birds A thorough study of the anatomy and physical makeup of animals and birds will provide very useful information for drawing and painting them. In almost all animals, every part serves a purpose and it is important that the artist be aware of these aspects.
Above: The layers of a bird's wing are analysed. These are similar to the human hand and arm.

Holman Hunt, 'The Dovecot'. A painting which incorporates a thorou

...nderstanding of the structure of the bird. When used in an atmospheric environment, this yields a subtle and evocative image.

Oil

1. Draw up the outline of the animal with a dark brown mixed from raw umber and black. Use a bristle brush and work freely to lay in the shapes.

2. Start to work into the head, sketching in the features with the tip of the brush and blocking in the colors of skin and fur.

WHILE THE ARTIST may use a natural history subject to successfully capture the essential characteristics of the subject, it may also be used as a vehicle for creating a dramatic picture.

In this painting, the background colors are part of the range used to paint the animals. Although this provides a close harmony in the whole image, the tones must be handled carefully, or the figures will merge into the background. The dark colors of the animals are a rich texture compared with the solid black behind. The flat pink color of the floor is modified and enlivened with a pattern of shadowy color.

Oil paint is a particularly suitable medium for this subject, as it can be blended and streaked to create an impression of soft fur. It is important to study the color carefully. Dark brown fur will have tints and lights which can be used to enrich the painting.

As a starting point, sketch out the forms loosely with a broad bristle brush but allow the overall shapes to emerge gradually in patches of color, treating each shape as a solid mass.

Materials

Surface
9oz cotton duck stretched and primed

Size
30in × 30in (75cm × 75cm)

Tools
Nos 3 and 6 flat bristle brushes
No 8 round sable brush
1in (2.5cm) decorators' brush
Wooden studio palette
1in (2.5cm) masking tape

Colors

Black	Cadmium yellow
Burnt sienna	Cobalt blue
Burnt umber	Raw sienna
Cadmium red	White

Medium
Turpentine

Working from sketch · blocking in tones · face details

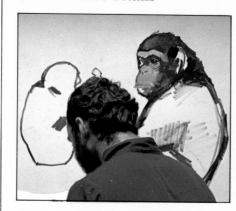

When painting or drawing animals, it is usually easier for the artist to make rough sketches from the live subject which are later used as reference for the finished work. Here the artist is working from a sketch pad.

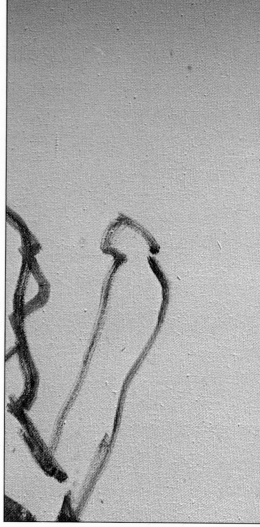

After the artist has roughed in the general shapes and positions of the animals, he begins to develop the faces. Using a large brush and color mixtures thinned with turpentine, he blocks in general color areas, scrubbing the paint into the surface and allowing these tones to blend with the black underpainting.

3. Use a sable brush to build up detail, developing the tonal structure of the head. Block in the whole shape of the body loosely with thin paint and a large brush.

4. Work up the color over the image with pinks and browns, strengthening the dark tones. Lay a thin layer of paint over the shape of the second animal.

5. Paint freely into both shapes, gradually improving the details of the form and at the same time intensifying the tonal contrasts. *(continued overleaf)*

Working over the damp under-painting, the artist begins to develop the details of the animal's face. Using a small sable brush and a thick paint mixture, he works over the initial black underpainting, darkening and refining. It is better to work over a damp surface as errors can be either scraped off or blended into the wet surface.

6. Fill in background color with a layer of thin paint. Use masking tape to make a straight line across the canvas and paint into the outlines to correct the shapes.

7. Dab in a multi-coloured texture over the plain area of floor, overlaying dots of red, pink, blue and yellow.

8. Scumble a thin layer of color over the patterning and thicken it gradually so that some areas of colored dots show through. Brush in solid black across background.

Spattering · putting in background

After the stippled background has been allowed to dry, the artist works with a decorators' brush, loosely blocking in color.

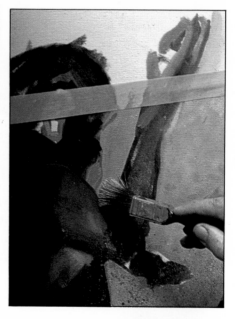

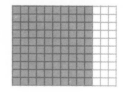

Right: An interesting paint texture can be created by spattering and stippling with a paint brush. The brush should be fairly large, stiff, and dry. The paint consistency is determined by the density of tone desired: the thicker the paint, the stronger the tone and larger the spatter. Above: The overall effect of the surface can be seen in detail. By overlaying a number of colors, from a distance the area will appear to blend into a continuous tone.

9. Draw back into the details of the face with a fine brush, adjusting the shapes and colors. Enrich the black and brown of the fur to give it texture and sheen.

10. Mask off the black background and work across with another layer of color to intensify the dark tone.

11. Draw up light brown shapes on the pink floor to suggest cast shadows. Finish off with white highlights in the fur.

TAKE TIME setting up a still life as the arrangement of the subject is entirely within your control. Move the objects around and consider the overall appearance from different viewpoints. Remember that the full freshness of flowers will not last long and natural light will change gradually during a day's work. Be prepared to work quickly and observe the subject extremely closely throughout the painting process.

Oil paint is the best medium for this type of subject. It keeps its true color as it dries, unlike watercolor which loses brilliance. It also mixes more subtly than acrylics so it is the most suitable medium to describe the range of vivid color and veiled, shadowy hues in the subject.

To establish the basic shapes and tones the composition is first drawn up in monochrome with layers of thin paint. The color is then built up gradually over the underpainting, initially modified by the tonal drawing and gaining full clarity in the final stages. Working quickly in oils means laying the paint wet-into-wet so brushmarks must be light but confident in order to apply colors directly without mixing them on the canvas. Thicken the paint slightly at each stage, adding gel medium where necessary. To make corrections, lift the paint carefully with a clean rag and rework the shapes. Check the drawing and color values continually as the painting evolves.

Materials

Surface
Prepared canvas board

Size
16in × 20in (40cm × 50cm)

Tools
Nos 3 and 6 flat bristle brushes
No 5 filbert
Sheet of glass or palette
Rags

Colors

Alizarin crimson	Permanent rose
Cadmium lemon	Prussian blue
Chrome oxide	Ultramarine blue
Chrome yellow	Vermilion
Cobalt blue	Viridian

Mediums
Rectified spirits of turpentine
Linseed oil
Gel medium

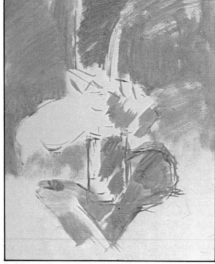

1. Use a flat bristle brush and cobalt blue paint to sketch in the basic lines of the composition. Thin the paint with turpentine and block in broad areas.

2. Strengthen dark tones with alizarin crimson, forming a purple cast over the blue. Draw into the pattern of shapes in more detail.

4. Work on the flowers, drawing in small shapes of red, pink and white. Vary the tone and density of the colors to suggest the form.

5. Refine the drawing with the tip of the brush and lay blocks of color with the bristles flat on the canvas.

7. Brighten the color of the leaves with light green, giving them more definition against the background. Lighten the table top with a layer of warm brown.

8. Brush over the background with a thin layer of blue mixed with a little red. Work over the blues in the foreground with a full range of light and dark tones.

3. Work into the foliage and jar with patches of green, mixing in touches of yellow and crimson. Paint in the background with brown and grey.

6. Bring up the tones of the white and pink flowers, applying the paint more thickly. Add details to the greens in the jar, mixing in yellow and white to vary the colors.

9. Apply small dabs of light color to the flowers, showing the forms in more detail. Work into the leaves behind with yellow and white, bringing out the shapes clearly.

Developing flower shapes

After the initial underpainting is completed in blues and greens, the artist blocks in flower shapes in a thin wash of red.

Working back into the flowers with a small bristle-brush to heighten dark and light contrasts.

PAINTING OR drawing animals can be very different from working from the human figure. Because animals are rarely still, drawing or painting them is often an excellent exercise in learning how to work quickly to capture their essential characteristics. If, however, this proves impossible, photographs or pictures can be used as reference material instead of a live subject.

To translate the animal's movement into the painting, pick out characteristic curves and angles in the body and legs. Watch the animal carefully as it moves, looking for repeated movements. Utilize the texture of your brushstrokes to describe thick fur, feathers, or other textures and lay in small touches of color in the earth tones to enliven the overall image. Keep the background simple to focus attention on the color and patterns within the animal.

It can be interesting to use more than one animal in a painting, as the artist can then show more than one position, movement, or type of behaviour. Again, photographs, other pictures or rough sketches made 'on location' can be used as a base, with the various animals or positions of the same animal being combined into the final picture.

Materials

Surface
Prepared canvas board

Size
20in × 24in (50cm × 60cm)

Tools
Willow charcoal
Nos 5 and 7 flat bristle brushes
No 5 filbert bristle brush
Sheet of glass or palette
Tissue or rag

Colors

Black	Cadmium yellow
Burnt sienna	Gold ochre
Burnt umber	Ultramarine blue
Cadmium red	Yellow ochre

Medium
Turpentine

1. Draw up the outline shape in charcoal. Block in basic areas of tone with yellow ochre and blue-black.

2. Sketch in the pattern of stripes in blue-black, using a small bristle brush. Scrub in thin layers of color over the whole picture.

3. Work quickly over the shape of the animal with yellow, burnt sienna and white laying color into the black pattern. Angle the brush marks to accentuate form.

4. Adjust the proportions of the drawing and the division of the picture plane. Strengthen the blacks and heighten the colors, adding touches of red and blue.

5. Develop the tonal range in the background, spreading the paint with a rag. Work with black and brown to make a dense area of shadow.

6. Continue to work up the colors, dabbing in the shapes with a bristle brush, well loaded with paint to make a rich texture.

Blocking in background · lightening

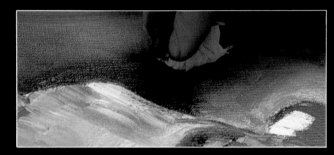

The artist rubs the background color into the surface with a tissue or piece of rag, to lighten the tone and pick up excess moisture.

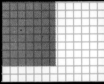

Using a thin wash of yellow ochre and black thinned with turpentine, the artist very loosely blocks in the background area, scrubbing the paint into the surface.

ONCE THE form and proportions of this painting were established in the initial drawing, the formal qualities of design, color, and texture became the major areas of interest. A study of the progress of this painting shows that the artist has made continual adjustments to the tones and colors, developing the image from a basic overall view rather than copying directly.

The paint surface is built up layer upon layer, with thin glazes first rubbed into the surface of the board. Thick impasto is applied with brushes and palette knives in craggy blocks of broken color or smooth opaque sweeps. Although the range of color is deliberately limited to exploit the tonal scale, the greys are varied across a wide range which contrast warm yellow hues and neutral or cool bluish tones. Areas of strong color, such as the pinks and reds of the pig's head, are established with the initial glazing then gradually covered and reglazed in the final stages.

The painting should be left to dry out at intervals as if the oil is laid on very thickly the paint will crack as it dries. The surface must be dry before the glazes are applied or the colors will merge and the clear sheen of the thin color will be lost.

Materials

Surface
Prepared canvas board

Size
24in × 20in (60cm × 50cm)

Tools
No 7 sable round brush
No 8 flat bristle brush
No 16 flat ox-ear brush
Assorted palette knives
Palette

Colors
Alizarin crimson	Ivory black
Burnt sienna	Payne's grey
Cadmium yellow	Prussian blue
Carmine	White
Cerulean blue	Prussian blue oil pastel

Mediums
Linseed oil
Turpentine

1. Draw the composition with Prussian blue oil pastel. Work over the drawing and block in tones with thinned Payne's grey with a No 16 brush.

2. Wash in layers of thin color – carmine and burnt sienna – over the table, the pig's head and the background, using the No 16 brush.

3. Mix cool, warm and neutral greys and spread thick paint over the background walls with palette knives and brushes. Work under the pig's head with white.

4. Work over the whole painting with impastoed layers of solid, textured color. Develop the form of the pig's head with pink, grey and white using a No 8 brush.

5. Continue to build up the layers of paint adjusting the tones of each shape until the whole surface is covered in cool and warm greys.

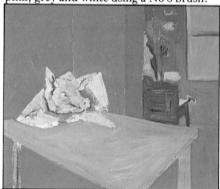

6. With a No 7 brush, draw into the pig's head with thick black lines and lighten the tone with palette knife and white paint. Rework the background tones.

7. Work over the forms with thin glazes of yellow-brown and dark grey, spread with rags.

8. Darken the tone of the whole work with thin layers of liquid glazes made from paint and linseed oil. Lay in bright pink and yellow tones over the pig's head.

Blocking in shapes · developing details

With a small bristle brush and ochre paint, the artist is here touching in the figure in the background.

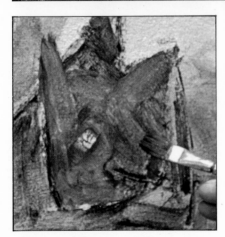

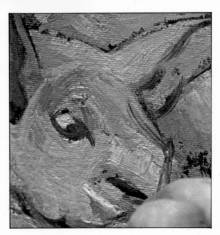

Working with a large sable brush and thinned paint, the artist blocks in general color tones, rubbing the paint into the surface.

After the reddish underpainting has been allowed to dry, the artist begins to develop the pig's head in broad strokes of pale pinks and greys.

When the artist has modelled the head to satisfaction, a small sable brush and dark paint are used to put back in outlines and details.

Acrylic

ILLUSTRATING ACRYLIC'S flexibility and adaptability, the artist has here used a combination of traditional watercolor and oil painting techniques. Stretched watercolor paper can be used with acrylics, as can sable watercolor brushes. The method used is very much a traditional oil painting technique; the artist uses an underpainting from which to create colors and tones.

The major advantage in using acrylics lies in the fact that the artist need not work from dark to light, but can constantly alter and work from both light to dark and dark to light. In some areas the artist has used traditional watercolor techniques such as the wash. By adding white to a color rather than thinning it opacity can be attained and the brush and paint maneuvered for detail work.

Materials

__Surface__
Heavy watercolor paper stretched on board

__Size__
18in × 14in (45cm × 35cm)

__Tools__
Nos 2 and 6 sable watercolour brushes
Palette or dishes
Rags
2B pencil

__Colors__

Black	Gold ochre
Burnt sienna	Lemon yellow
Cadmium yellow medium	Raw umber
Cadmium yellow pale	Vermilion
Chrome green	White

__Medium__
Water

1. Stretch a piece of watercolor paper and after lightly roughing in the subject, apply a thin wash of gold ochre around the subject with a No 6 brush.

2. Using chrome green, begin to lay in the general leaf color varying the tone by making the paint more or less transparent.

3. Mixing vermilion and burnt sienna, describe the branch. Mix lemon yellow and vermilion and put in the apples. Add umber to ochre and block in shadow area.

4. Mix white with gold ochre and block in the area of the background not in shadow. Mix a small amount of black with chrome green and darken the leaf tones.

5. To create lighter leaf tones, mix white, yellow ochre and green. Use pure vermilion to put in darker fruit tones.

6. Mix gold ochre and raw umber to strengthen the shadow area under the branch. Work over existing leaf tones with a darker, more opaque green.

7. Mix chrome green, yellow and white and with a No 2 brush define leaf details, using the underpainting to create the veins in the leaves.

8. Using the same ochre and umber mixture, heighten the shadow under the branch. Thin with water to make a variety of tones rather than adding white.

Developing and refining leaves

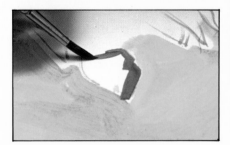

After putting in the background color, the artist blocks in the leaves with a fine sable brush.

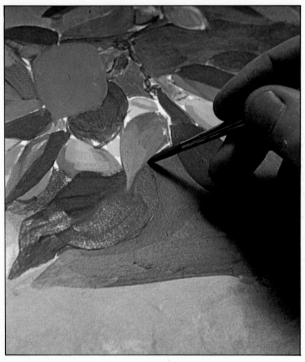

With a mixture of chrome green and white and a small brush, the artist cleans up outlines of the leaves.

THE COMPLEX COLORING of zebras is the basic structure for a semi-abstract composition in this painting. The formal qualities of the pattern which include minimal color and high tonal contrasts were selected from black and white photographs which served to emphasize the two-dimensionality of the design.

The forms create a rhythmic framework of light and dark shapes designed to cut across the picture plane in a complex, irregular structure. To vary the color scheme, a warm yellow ochre and cool cobalt blue are mixed into the basic whites and greys. Broad blocks of color surrounding the forms do not indicate a particular environment but are used as a feature of the overall composition.

You will need to make continual adjustments to the colors to arrive at a satisfactory arrangement of the tones. This can be done directly on the canvas, as acrylic paint dries rapidly enough to make overpainting immediately possible. Never try to scrape off partially dry acrylic, however, as it dries with a thick rubbery skin which tears away from the surface. Simply allow the paint to dry and cover any errors with another layer of color.

Materials

<u>Surface</u>
Prepared canvas board

<u>Size</u>
18in × 16in (45cm × 40cm)

<u>Tools</u>
Nos 3, 5 flat bristle brushes
No 10 flat synthetic brush
No 6 round sable brush
Palette or plate

<u>Colors</u>

Black	Vermilion
Cobalt blue	White
Payne's grey	Yellow ochre
Raw umber	

<u>Medium</u>
Water

1. Establish the structure of the composition drawing in simple outline shapes with black paint and a No 5 brush.

2. Work over the forms in black and white constructing the pattern of the stripes and block in broad areas of background tone with a No 10 brush.

3. With a No 5 brush, develop tones using yellow ochre as an intermediate color. Keep to simple shapes, varying the brushstrokes to make thin and thick lines.

4. Make alterations to the shapes by outlining in red with a No 6 brush. Strengthen the contrast of light and dark, working across the forms.

5. Redraft the pattern of lines using the No 6 brush for fine lines and the No 3 brush for thick black strokes.

6. Build up variations in the light tones, adding a little cobalt blue to the greys to offset the yellow and pure white. Extend the pattern across the whole image.

7. Work on the background tones, trying out different combinations of light and dark tones.

8. Block in background and foreground shapes with thick color, using the warm-toned yellow to highlight the black and white.

Developing light areas

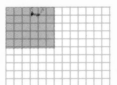

After the initial shapes and outlines of the zebras have been described, the artist here works back into the lighter areas with a small brush and pure white paint.

Watercolor

THE WATERCOLOR techniques used for this painting are particularly well suited to the subject. A combination of loose transparent strokes with opaque white gouache produce an interesting contrast in both texture and tone.

The techniques used – working wet-in-wet and dry-brush – require that the painting be executed quickly and confidently. The process involves working from dark to light and from the general to the particular.

Tinted paper was chosen since it has a unifying and reinforcing effect on the painting. When the color of the paper is used as a 'color' within the subject, as demonstrated in the head of the bird, the contrast in color and texture both heighten the interest in the subject and link it to its environment.

The method of painting is largely intuitive: you should try and let the painting develop independently and take advantage of the various movements of the paint on the surface. A careful combination of control and a willingness to take chances is required and you should learn to take advantage of 'accidents' and use them to express the unique qualities of the picture.

Materials

Surface
Heavy watercolor paper stretched on board

Size
15in × 22in (37.5cm × 55cm)

Tools
Board
Gummed tape
Nos 1 and 2 sable watercolor brushes
Tissues or rags

Colors
Alizarin crimson	Payne's grey
Cadmium red medium	Prussian blue

Medium
Water

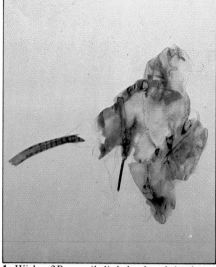

1. With a 2B pencil, lightly sketch in the subject. With a No 2 sable brush, lay in a thin wash of burnt umber, blue, and alizarin crimson to define the shape of the bird.

2. Mix a small amount of white gouache with blue and lay this over the undercolors, thinning with water. Put in dark areas with Payne's grey.

3. With a No 1 brush, mix white gouache with blue and touch in feathers with a light, directional stroke. Add more blue and describe feather texture in the wing.

Underpainting· feathering with brush tip

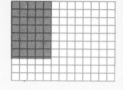

(**A**, above) The artist puts in a cool underpainting with a wet wash and large sable brush.

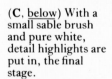

(**B**, above) Using the dry-brush technique, the artist describes a feather texture in the neck.

(**C**, below) With a small sable brush and pure white, detail highlights are put in, the final stage.

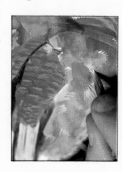

4. With the same brush mix an opaque mixture of Payne's grey and blue and carefully put in dark details of the wings, tail, and head.

5. With a clean, dry No 1 brush pick up a small amount of white gouache. Feather this onto the bird's breast and throat in a quick, flicking motion.

6. With a very thin wash of white gouache mixed with blue, quickly rough in the shadow area around the bird.

WATERCOLOR USES transparency to create both color and tone. For this reason white is not normally a part of the watercolorist's palette and thus the artist must rely on the various techniques and color mixes to achieve a successful picture. In this painting the variety of techniques illustrate the flexibility of the medium, as well as the skill required to use it to its best potential.

The demands of using watercolor require that the artist be able to anticipate what will happen in advance of putting the paint on the surface. This can be a hit or miss effort, especially when applying loose washes of color or letting colors bleed into one another. The artist has a certain amount of control over where and how the paint is applied, but once the brush touches the paper there is much that can happen which the artist will not be able to predict.

In this case, while care was taken to capture a true representation of the subject, the background was described in a more or less *ad hoc* manner, allowing paint and water to mix with no attempt to control its movement on the surface.

1. Mix a very wet wash of cadmium green and water and loosely define the leaf shapes with a No 6 brush.

2. With a small amount of cerulean blue and a No 2 brush, put in the dark areas of the flowers. Mix green and yellow ochre and lay in the dark areas of the leaves.

Materials

Surface
Stretched watercolor paper

Size
23in × 18in (57cm × 45cm)

Tools
Nos 2, 6, 10 sable brushes
1½ (3.75cm) housepainting brush
Palette

Colors
Black   Payne's grey
Cadmium green   Vermilion
Cerulean blue   Yellow ochre

Medium
Water

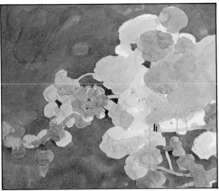

3. Mix a large, wet amount of Payne's grey, cerulean blue, and water. With a No 10 brush, put in the background. Keep the paint very wet as you work.

4. With a No 2 brush, develop dark tones of the leaves by mixing Payne's grey with green. Again, keep the mixture wet and let colours bleed into one another.

5. With a No 2 brush, apply details of stems and veins in pure Payne's grey.

Finished picture · creating leaf shapes · overpainting flowers

To bring the picture together and make it more interesting, in the final stages the artist concentrated on darkening and strengthening the overall image. The background was brought down to describe the foreground plane, and leaves and flowers were touched up with stronger tones.

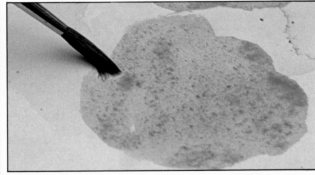

With a very wet wash of water and green, the artist describes the general leaf shapes. The wet paint is pulled out of these areas in thin strands to create the stems of the leaves.

With a small sable brush the artist is here touching in areas of deep red over the lighter underpainting. From a distance, this will give the flowers depth and texture.

ANY WATERCOLOR study of this kind is an exercise in drawing with color. In both objects, by carefully copying each detail of color and texture, the whole impression of the form slowly emerges. The shell is delicately tinged with red, yellow, and grey and the subtle tonal changes which occur as the light falls over the undulating surface are subtly indicated.

Lay in broad washes of basic color to show the simple form and contour of the objects. Pick out linear details such as the network of triangular shapes on the pine cone, drawing with the point of a small sable brush. Use thin washes of color to describe the pools of shadow and natural tints of the shell. Keep the paint smooth and liquid but do not overload the brush – the color should flow freely but not flood the drawing. The work should be dried before fine lines are added otherwise they will fan out and lose precision. Brush wet washes of color together to blend the hues and make the paint spread into soft, blurred shapes of variegated tone. Mix up a subtle range of browns and greys to vary the dark tones and drop in touches of pure color to highlight the surface patterns.

Materials

Surface
Thick cartridge paper

Size
13in × 15in (32cm × 37.5cm)

Tools
Nos 4, 8 sable round brushes
Palette

Colors
Black
Burnt sienna
Burnt umber
Cobalt blue

Gamboge yellow
Payne's grey
Scarlet lake

Medium
Water

1. Draw the shape of the pine cone with the tip of a No 4 brush and lay in a light wash of burnt umber. Vary the tone with touches of Payne's grey.

3. Develop the texture and pattern in each shape, drawing fine lines and small patches of color with the point of the brush in dark tones of grey and brown.

5. Lay thin washes of grey, brown and red into the shape of the shell with a No 8 brush.

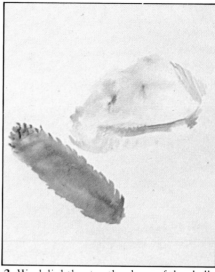

2. Work lightly over the shape of the shell following the local color. Pick out small surface details on both objects.

4. Strengthen the dark tone inside the mouth of the shell and continue to work over the pine cone, using the direction of the brushmarks to describe the forms.

6. Work over both objects with line and wash until the patterns are complete.

Pine cone details · shell tones

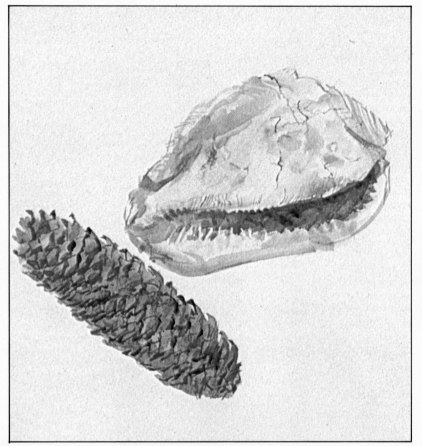

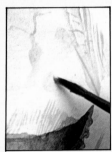

With a very faint mixture of water and paint, the subtle tones within the shell are brushed in.

With a very fine sable brush and burnt umber, the artist describes the details of the pine cone over the dry underpainting.

Pine cone details · shell tones

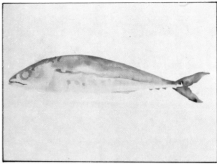

1. On a piece of stretched paper, dampen the shape of the fish with water. With a small sable brush put in a thin wash of blue and purple. Flood with brush and water.

2. Redampen the area to be worked on. With a fine brush and dryish paint, put in the head and spine details in Payne's grey letting this bleed into the other colors.

WATERCOLOR IS AT its best when used for subjects requiring sensitivity and delicacy. In this case, the use of watercolor goes far in developing an appropriate aqueous and 'watery' image.

The techniques used by the watercolorist are many and not a few are invented on the spot as the artist is working. There is no formula for creating a successful watercolor painting; however, the better acquainted the artist is with the nature of the medium, the more he will be able to pick and choose – and invent – the techniques most suitable to create an interesting and expressive picture.

In developing this picture, the artist has depended largely on two methods of painting. In some areas he has used the classical wet-into-wet technique – that is, flooding one area of color into another while still wet; in other areas he has laid down a small area of color and then flooded this with water. The combination of the two from the earlier techniques makes the finished painting more interesting than if it were limited to one type only. It is the combination of broad, loose areas of pale color contrasted with smaller, tighter areas of dark detail which give the subject its mystery and interest. Without this contrast and harmonious balance between loose and tight, dark and light, the picture would not be so successful in holding the observer's attention or capturing the essence of the subject.

Wet-in-wet · dark details the wash

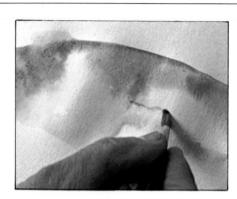

With a fine sable brush, the artist puts in fine lines of color over slightly damp paper.

Putting in dark details in the head with a dryish paint mixture. The color is then flooded with water and a clean brush to make it bleed.

Materials

Surface
Heavy watercolor paper stretched on board

Size
22in × 15in (55cm × 37.5cm)

Tools
Nos 2 and 6 sable watercolor brushes
Tissues or rags

Colors
Alizarin crimson	Payne's grey
Cadmium red medium	Prussian blue

Medium
Water

3. After allowing the previous layer to dry slightly, use a stronger and darker mixture of Payne's grey to further define the head.

4. Mix a thin wash of purple and yellow and apply lightly over the body of the fish. Blot with tissue if too wet.

5. Using the deep Payne's grey mixture and a small brush, put in the pattern on the back and heighten tail details.

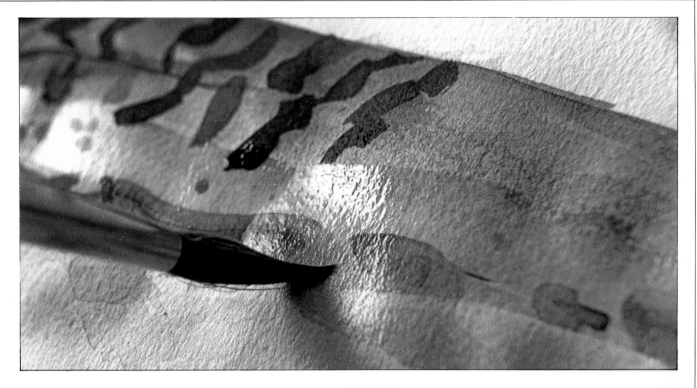

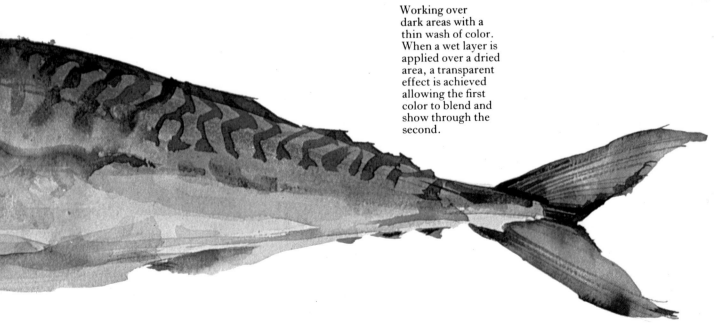

Working over dark areas with a thin wash of color. When a wet layer is applied over a dried area, a transparent effect is achieved allowing the first color to blend and show through the second.

Tempera

THE ORTHODOX tempera painter uses only the finest ground pigments, fresh hen's eggs, expensive and finely crafted brushes, and a surface polished to a marble-like finish. There are many artists however who use shorter and less expensive methods and obtain very satisfactory results. For example, with tubed watercolors and egg yolk, it is simple to create a successful tempera painting in as little time as it takes to do a drawing or watercolor painting.

Egg yolk is a viscous, sticky medium and behaves similarly when brushed on to a surface. Because it dries quickly, the artist must work quickly to avoid the brush dragging and pulling up the painted surface.

Although tempera dries quickly – quickly enough to cause problems – it will not dry to an impenetrable state immediately. Once partially dry, the artist can draw into the surface with a sharp tool, scratching back the paint to the surface. He can then either leave this clean or overpaint in thin glazes. This method of laying down paint, scratching back, and overlaying more paint can be continued almost indefinitely, varying the tone and modifying drawn lines or area of color.

Materials

Surface
Primed hardboard

Size
5.5in × 7in (14cm × 17.5cm)

Tools
No 2 sable watercolor brush
Plate or palette

Colors
Cadmium red light   Viridian
Cerulean blue   Yellow ochre
Chrome green

Mediums
Egg yolk
Water

1. Dip a No 2 brush into egg yolk and mix with viridian and chrome green. Quickly block in the leaf shapes using a downward stroke. Leave flower areas untouched.

2. Mix chrome green and yellow ochre with the egg and block in the leaf shapes. With only chrome green, draw in outlines and stems.

3. Using the same green, block in major dark areas with a light, vertical stroke. Allow to dry until sticky to the touch.

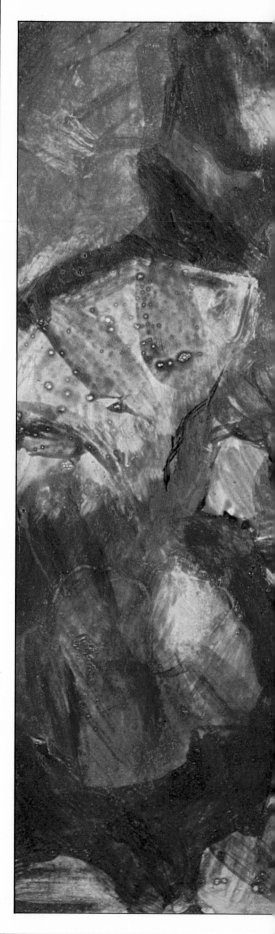

Finished picture detail

As a final step, the artist puts in thin streaks of pure cerulean blue to enliven the predominantly green surface.

4. With a knife or sharp tool, scratch through the paint surface drawing in the leaf outlines and hatch in small areas of highlight in the leaves.

5. With cadmium red and yolk, block in the flowers. When partly dry, scratch back the surface of the leaves in broad areas. Overlay with a wash of green and yolk.

6. With a deeper red, define flower shadows and with cerulean blue, put in the fine lines of blue in the darker shadow areas for contrast.

Gouache

BECAUSE OF their varied textures, colors, and shapes, plants can be an interesting subject for a painting.

To make an effective color study of one plant, arrange it in a well-lit position, preferably against a plain background. Sit far enough away to be able to see the whole form, as otherwise the shapes may become distorted in the drawing. You can move to take a closer look at the details whenever necessary. First draw the whole plant in outline and then start to apply colors. A successful rendering depends upon careful observation of the color relationships as a whole – each hue and tone is modified by its surroundings. Be prepared to make continual alterations to the colors and shapes.

In this example the initial drawing was made in charcoal. The soft, dusty black creates a strong structure for the work and is easy to correct or overpaint. Keep the charcoal drawing clean, or the fine black powder will mix into the paint and deaden the colors. Lay in thin colors at the start to establish general tones and then work over each shape to revise the colors and build up the pattern.

Materials

Surface
Stretched white cartridge paper

Size
15in × 19in (37.5cm × 47cm)

Tools
No 6 round sable brush
Willow charcoal
Plate or palette

Colors
Black	Olive green
Cadmium yellow medium	Raw umber
Cyprus green	Scarlet lake
May green	White

Medium
Water

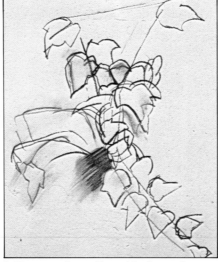

1. Draw up the outline with charcoal showing the shapes of the leaves and the stalks. Work freely, correcting where necessary by rubbing lightly over the lines.

3. Fill in the whole shape of each leaf. Draw the stalks of the plant in red using the tip of the brush.

5. Build up the image piece by piece with applied color, gradually adding to the detail and refining the shapes.

2. Brush away excess charcoal dust from the surface of the drawing and with a No 6 brush work into the leaves to show the green patterning.

4. Revise the drawing with charcoal and paint over alterations with white. Continue to develop the colors, putting in a darker tone behind the leaves.

6. Adjust the tones of the colors to draw out the natural contrasts. Complete each shape before moving onto the next.

Beginning to work · refining leaf shapes

Working with a small sable brush and pale green, the artist works directly over the sketch, blocking in tones.

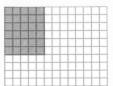

After the dark green of the leaves has dried, an opaque pale green is blocked in around these shapes.

Pastel

IN TERMS OF color, shape, and gesture, the subject for this picture is well suited to a pastel drawing as bold colors and sharp, gestural strokes are few of the many potential uses of pastel. Of course the technique used will determine the end result; if this picture had been executed with heavy blending, smudging and subtle color the results would be quite different.

The colors used are basically complementary: red, orange and pink; blue, purple and green. It is worth remembering that color is created by light, and color will always reflect and bounce off neighboring colors. The artist has exploited this by using a complementary color within a predominant color area. Thus there are touches of red in the purple flowers, and touches of purple in the red and orange flowers. The dark blue used to describe the stems and shadow areas works as a contrast to both the purple, blue, and red, intensifying and adding depth to the overall picture.

The composition was purposely arranged to give a feeling of closeness. The white of the paper works in stark contrast to the densely clustered stems and flowers in the bottom left corner and the directional strokes serve to lead the eye upward and across the page.

Materials

Surface
Pastel paper

Size
16in × 20in (40cm × 50cm)

Tools
Tissue or rag
Willow charcoal
Fixative

Colors

Blue-green	Orange
Cadmium red medium	Pale blue
Cadmium yellow medium	Pink
Cobalt blue	Prussian blue
Dark green	White
Light green	

1. After roughing in the flower shapes with charcoal, lightly sketch in the flowers in pink, red, and purple and the stems in light and dark greens.

2. With a small piece of tissue, blend the color tones of the flowers. With pale blue, work back into the purple flowers describing the petals with sharp strokes.

A method of blending is to use a small piece of tissue. Unlike a finger, the tissue will both blend colors and pick up the pastel, thus lightening the tone.

Pastel marks can either be left as clean strokes or blended into subtle gradations of tone and color. Here the artist is blending within the flowers, mixing the orange and pink.

Using the tip of a pastel, the artist describes stem and leaf shapes with a quick, loose motion

3. With cadmium red and orange, emphasize the petal shapes with sharp strokes. With dark blue, define stems with the same sharp, directional strokes.

4. With purple pastel, put a heavier layer down within the blue flowers. Use the same color to put in additional leaf and stem shapes with a loose stroke.

5. Returning to the flowers, apply deeper tones with more pressure. Add touches of red to the purple flowers. Create flower centers with yellow in the pink flowers.

Finished picture blending · stem and leaf shapes

To finish the picture (<u>right</u>), the artist continued to develop strong dark areas with blue. As a final step, a tissue was used to pick up loose color and blend into the right hand corner.

PERFECTING THE techniques needed to draw effectively in pastel takes time. As pastels are loose and powdery, the sticks must be carefully manipulated to achieve any degree of precision. If you work on tinted paper, the light tones may be handled as positive, strong colors while the tint adds depth to the overall tone of the work.

Outlines, where used, should be light and sketchy, merely providing a guideline to be eventually overlaid by areas of color. Spray the drawing with fixative whenever necessary to keep the colors bright and stable. Overlay layers of color with light strokes of the pastels to create soft, intermediary tones.

Materials

Surface
Blue pastel paper

Size
11in × 15in (27cm × 37cm)

Tools
Fixative

Colors
Black	Orange
Cobalt blue	Pink
Dark and light green	White
Dark and light red	Yellow

1. Loosely sketch in the basic position of the bird with red and orange pastels. Draw the crest of the head in white.

2. Work over the drawing with vigorous, scribbled marks, contrasting the orange and red of the bird against green and yellow in the background.

3. Construct a solid impression of shape, drawing into the form with white and black. Work into the background with light tones.

4. Strengthen outlines on the bird in black and lay in a dark green behind. Add small details in blue and white.

5. Strengthen the colour over the whole image, showing shadows and highlights. Overlay scribbled patches of different colors.

6. Spray the drawing with fixative and let it dry. Reinforce the red shapes, giving the form more definition. Work up linear details in the background.

Developing general shapes and tones · highlighting

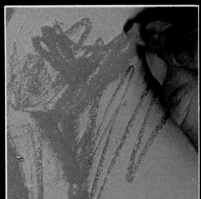

Here the artist begins to block in the color of the bird with a very loose, scribbling motion.

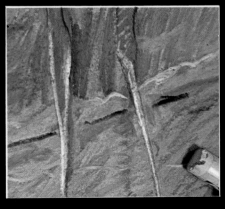

With pale yellow, the artist moves across the picture putting in loose lines of highlight.

Pencil

WASH AND LINE illustrates the ability of mixed media to capture an image both simply and directly. By a skillfull use of line and carefully placed touches of wash, the artist is able to reduce the subject to its bare essentials, creating a picture which is fresh and simple in style.

How to decide upon the ratio of line to wash, and vice versa, takes practice and a keen eye. There are no hard and fast rules but, in general, it is best to keep the image as clear and uncluttered as possible. The temptation to cover the surface with many colors and techniques is a common one; it takes practice, restraint, and a critical eye to put into the picture only what is absolutely essential to best express the subject.

A good reason for resisting the temptation to cover the page is that often the plain white surface can emphasize a line or dab of color far more than any techniques or additional colors can. It is the use of contrast – the broad white or tinted paper contrasting with the sharp edge of a line or subtle wash of color – which serves to emphasize and draw attention to the image. The emptiness and cleanness of a few well-chosen lines and dots of color, when combined with the untouched surface can create an image of eye-catching simplicity.

Materials

Surface
Thick cartridge paper

Size
26in × 18in (65cm × 45cm)

Tools
4B pencil
Putty eraser

Colors
Gold ochre watercolor

Medium
Water

The final touches of detail are put in with a soft, dark pencil.

1. Begin by putting a small amount of gold ochre directly on to a small piece of rag.

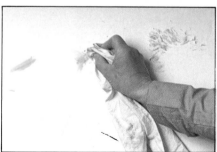

2. Rub the gold ochre on to the surface to create general color areas. Use your finger or fingers to draw with the paint and create feathered textures similar to fur.

Feathering · drawing in shapes · details

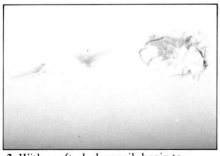

With a dense stroke, the artist is here seen working over the yellow wash to put in the general shape of the lion.

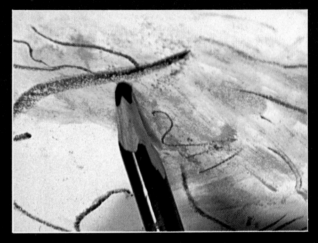

A feathered texture can be achieved by using the fingers to lightly touch the paint on to the surface. Do not use too much paint on the rag and do not dilute with turpentine.

3. With a soft, dark pencil, begin to describe the lion's head over the gold ochre paint. Vary the thickness and width of the line.

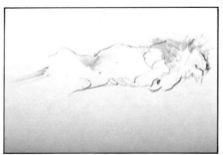

4. With the same pencil, continue down the body of the lion with a light, flowing stroke.

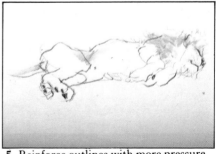

5. Reinforce outlines with more pressure. Put in dark details in the head and feet.

A SKULL is a good subject for a pencil drawing as it has a fluid and well-defined outline. The overall structure however is quite complex, containing a variety of linear and tonal details. The smooth, rounded dome of the skull demands subtle changes of tone which contrast with the dense, black shadows in the sockets of the eyes, nose and mouth.

The forms are represented by overlaid layers of shading and crosshatching married with crisp lines outlining the shapes and describing small fissures in the surface. Allow the image to emerge gradually by first developing the structure as a broad view of the whole shape and then breaking down each area to show details.

Arrange the subject carefully when you start a drawing to make sure it presents an interesting view which shows clearly the qualities to be described by the drawing medium. Use an HB pencil in the early stages moving on to a softer 2B to reinforce the lines and dark tones. If you work slowly and logically over the form it may not be necessary to use an eraser, but be prepared to make continual minor adjustments as the drawing develops. Vary the direction of the hatched lines to correspond to the network of curves and cavities. In this case, other bones have been drawn in to establish a horizontal plane and so the shape is not isolated.

Materials

Surface
Thick cartridge paper

Size
18in × 20in (45cm × 50cm)

Tools
HB and 2B pencils
Putty eraser
Fixative

1. Use an HB pencil to sketch in the outline of the skull and the sockets of the eyes and nose. Work loosely with line and light hatching, strengthening the shape.

2. Extend the outline shape and start to hatch in dark shadows, working the pencil in different directions to intensify the tones.

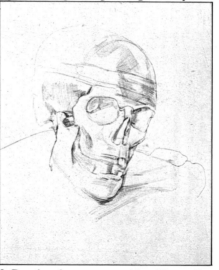

3. Develop the structure with a 2B pencil. Work over the whole drawing blocking in small shapes and improving the definition of the contours.

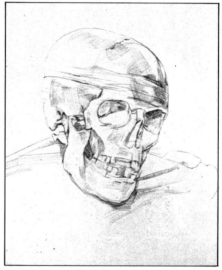

4. Continue to build up the form in more detail, drawing small shapes of the teeth and jaw socket. Use an eraser where necessary to make corrections.

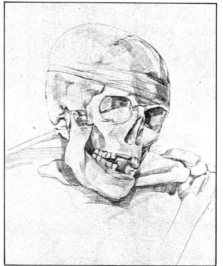

5. Strengthen the outlines and work over dark tones with crosshatched lines to give depth and bring out the full volume of the form.

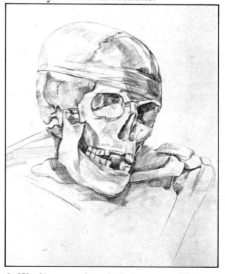

6. Work across the whole image making minor adjustments in the tonal balance and reinforcing the lines where appropriate to clarify the overall structure.

Crosshatching the eye area

The artist is seen here working into the eye cavity with a soft, dark pencil. Note the use of crosshatching to create depth. The darker the hatching, the more the shape will appear to recede.

WILLOW CHARCOAL IS often used for preliminary sketches for paintings but it is also an exciting medium in its own right. The most enjoyable aspect of drawing with willow charcoal is its responsiveness to touch and stroke. Another important feature is that it is easily erased – the artist can put down very intense, black areas and either lighten or remove these entirely with a putty eraser or tissue. The line achieved with willow charcoal is soft and fluid but by no means weak. A wide variety of tones and textures can be achieved through the use of line, tone, blending, and erasing.

The picture here is a good example of the various techniques available. The artist has relied purely on tone, texture, and stroke to give the animal weight and to distinguish it from its surroundings. The elephant is described in soft, blended tones, while the background is created with bold, directional strokes each offsetting the other.

The picture developed through a constant movement between dark and light areas and lines. A dark area is put in, lightened, and then the artist again returned to the dark areas. As seen in the steps, there was a constant progression from light to dark and back again, but within this there was a constant adjustment and readjustment of shadow and highlight, soft and bold, blended areas and linear strokes.

Materials

Surface
Rough drawing paper

Size
23.5in × 22in (59cm × 55cm)

Tools
2B pencil
Medium and light willow charcoal
Putty eraser
Tissues
Fixative

1. After putting in the general shape and composition of the drawing in light pencil, redraw the outline of the animal and background with fine willow charcoal.

2. Using the side of a piece of light charcoal, rough in shadow areas of animal. With a piece of medium charcoal, quickly sketch in the background.

Erasing highlights · laying in tones

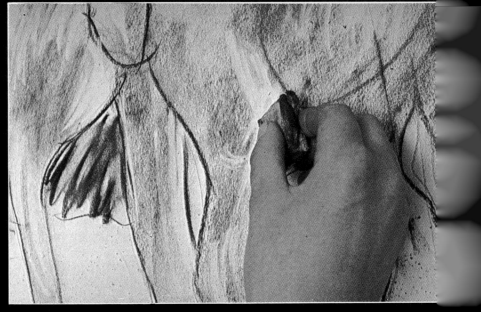

In the first few steps, broad areas of tone are laid down using the side of the charcoal.

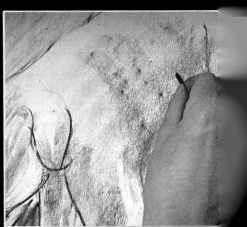

A putty eraser may be used to create highlights. Here the artist is erasing back through the charcoal, blocking in light areas.

3. With medium charcoal, work back into the shadow areas of the elephant in loose strokes. Blend area around eye with finger. With putty eraser, erase highlights.

4. Develop darks in background by putting down strokes and blending. Rework outline of elephant. Blend shadow areas beneath with tissue or finger.

5. With heavy, gestural strokes, put in background. Strengthen darks in elephant and blend. Use putty eraser to clean up whites and highlight areas.

Pen and ink

THE LOOSE LINE and confident strokes which experienced pen and ink artists achieve are acquired more by a relaxed attitude than superior drawing talents. More than any other medium, if the artist is worried about his strokes, the pen and ink drawing will immediately reveal his concern; the artist must make a conscious effort to overcome a desire to control or inhibit the line of the pen and the flow of the ink.

The artist has here achieved an informal sketch with little detail or careful rendering. The strokes are loose, flowing, casual. While there are many artists who consider any form of correction wrong, it is perfectly acceptable to correct a pen and ink drawing, as the artist has done here, with white gouache. On the other hand, as it is impossible to draw over lumps of white paint without interrupting the flow of the line, massive correcting may destroy the naturalness of the picture.

Materials

Surface
Smooth cartridge paper

Size
6.5in × 9in (16cm × 22cm)

Tools
2B pencil
Dip pen
Medium nib
No 2 sable brush

Colors
Black waterproof India ink
White designer's gouache

Medium
Water

1. With a 2B pencil, roughly sketch in the horse's head and area to be worked within.

2. Develop the eyes with fine crosshatching. If any area of the drawing becomes too dense, it may be corrected with a small sable brush and gouache.

3. Work down the head indicating musculature with a light, diagonal stroke.

4. Block in the surrounding area with broad, dark strokes. To create a darker tone, work back over these strokes in another direction.

5. Put in the darkest areas with a scribbling motion and plenty of ink. Redefine the outlines of the head with a dense, dark line.

6. Work back into the head and surrounding area with crosshatching to create darker tones and shadow areas.

Beginning details · correcting

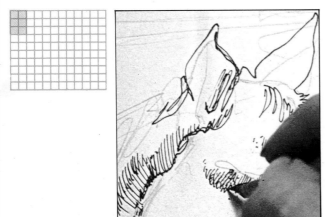

With a very fine
nib, the artist puts in
details around the
eye.

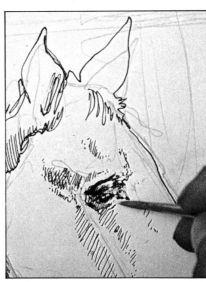

Small areas of ink
can be corrected by
using a small brush
and white designers'
gouache. This can
be used for small
corrections only.

PEN AND INK is considered best suited for tight detail work and densely cross-hatched drawing; however, it is just as possible to use it for loose and informal work. When what are often considered 'mistakes' – such as blending, running, smudging and blotting – are incorporated into the technique, a pen and ink drawing can take on new meaning.

In the drawing here, the artist has taken advantage of all these factors and incorporated them without losing either the strength of the drawing or the subject. Little attempt has been made to control the line of the pen – something many artists struggle hard to achieve – but, instead, the artist has let the nib catch and jump across the page without interference. While working, the artist's eye rarely left the subject; there was a direct line between what was seen and what appeared on the paper, resulting in a series of lines and marks which possibly suggest the subject better than careful and analytical rendering would have.

When the artist's goal is to capture the essence of the subject rather than creating a nice drawing, the attempt to control will hinder rather than help. In which case it is much better to assume an open attitude and allow the hand to follow the eye naturally and without interference.

Materials

Surface
Stretched white cartridge paper

Size
14in × 19.5in (35cm × 49cm)

Tools
No 2 sable brush
Dip pen
Medium nib

Colors
April green
Black
Blue
Red

Medium
Water

Using side of the pen · finishing details

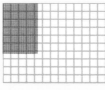

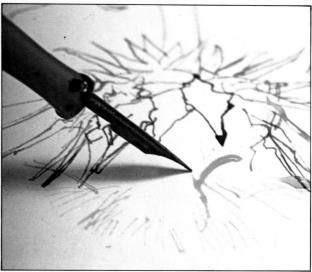

Although a medium nib is being used, a thick line is produced by turning the pen on its side and pulling it across the surface.

The artist is here describing the final details of the thistle over the light green wash. An irregular, jagged line is achieved by loading the nib with ink and letting it drag across the surface.

1. To dilute the color, dip the pen in water and then green ink and begin to describe the general outline of the plant. Repeat with red and black inks.

2. Move down the thistle with green ink letting the pen create a rough outline. Do not attempt a careful rendering but let it drag across the paper.

3. Dip the pen in water and then blue ink. Begin to put in the flower shape with quick, directional strokes. Dip the pen in black ink and redraw the outline.

4. Continue with the black ink working back over the lines previously drawn in green. Again, do not attempt a smooth line but let the nib catch on the paper.

5. When the drawing is partially dry, mix a light wash of green and water and with a No 2 sable brush quickly block in the general color areas.

6. Dilute blue ink and work into the flower with the same brush. With a clean dry brush and pure undiluted ink, put in the leaf shapes.